First FACES

by SNAZAROO

To find out more about Snazaroo products visit our website at
www.Snazaroo.com or telephone us on
+44 (0) 1643 707659.

KING*f*ISHER

KINGFISHER
Kingfisher Publications Plc
New Penderel House
283-288 High Holborn
London WC1V 7HZ
www.kingfisherpub.com

First published by Kingfisher Publications 1995
10 9 8 7 6 5 4
Copyright © Kingfisher Publications Plc

A CIP catalogue record for this book
is available from the British Library.

ISBN 978 1 85697 307 6
SNAZ/0407/EDK/FR/CS150/F

Editor: Jilly MacLeod
Designer: Karin Ambrose
Cover designer: Terry Woodley
Photographer: Roger Krump
Illustrations on pages 30-31: Stephen Holmes
Face painters: Lauren Cornell, Wilhelmina Barnden,
Helen Buckingham, Sandy Downer, Mark Mossman,
Kirsten Stewart and Janet Tapp.

The publishers would like to thank the following
children for acting as models in this book: Louise
Ahearn, Anna Binding, Charlene Champion, Kelvin
Champion, Simon Champion, Catherine Downer,
Jessica Downer, Laura Downer, Gemma Jeffs, Jenny
Mossman, Asher Smith, Christian Smith, Nichol Smith,
Sam Tapp, Stuart Walker, Matthew
Walsh, Tian Walsh, Yoliswa Walsh,
Gareth Watts, Melissa Watts
and James Wigglesworth.

CONTENTS

GETTING STARTED

Face painting is great fun to do and so easy to learn. With a little practice, you'll soon be able to create any of the fantastic face-painting designs shown in this book in less than five minutes!

Before you begin, read the next four pages carefully so you'll know what materials you will need and how to use them. Most importantly, look at the safety tips shown in the box on the next page.

WHICH PAINTS TO USE

The best paints to buy are water-based face paints. These are quick and easy to put on. They also dry fast and won't smudge (as long as you don't get them wet). You can even use them in your hair. Water-based face paints are also easy to remove – just rinse off with a little soap and water.

You can buy face paints in single pots or in palettes which contain several colours. Face paints are sold in craft shops, department stores and shops that sell theatrical costumes and make-up.

To add a touch of sparkle, you can also buy special glitter paints in bright colours.

BRUSHES AND SPONGES

You will also need some brushes and sponges. Buy a selection of brushes of different thicknesses. Special brushes made of sable or a material called toray are best, although nylon brushes will work perfectly well.

Buy make-up sponges made of soft foam for sponging on the base coat. You can also use baby sponges cut into wedge shapes.

USEFUL EXTRAS

Other useful things you will need include a towel, plenty of tissues or moisture wipes, a mirror and lots of water for cleaning your brushes and sponges.

If you can't find the materials you need, write to us for a mail order catalogue at this address:

Snazaroo
The Old Forge
Park Lane
Carhampton
Somerset TA24 6NL
United Kingdom

SAFETY FIRST

• Always use non-toxic face paints (paints that won't harm your skin).

• Never use face paints on someone with a skin problem or an allergy. If you're not sure, test your friend first with a small patch of face paint on his or her wrist.

• Never paint too close to the eyes, especially with a brush.

• Never use the type of glitter paints that are designed for painting on paper.

HERE'S HOW

Follow these few simple steps and you'll be able to paint wonderful faces every time.

BEFORE YOU BEGIN
First, sit your model down in front of you on a comfortable chair.

If you like, you can put a towel round his or her shoulders. This will stop you getting any paint on your model's clothes. Then tie back long hair so that it doesn't get in the way.

You should always paint on clean dry skin, so wipe your model's face clean with a moisture wipe or tissue.

Lay your materials out beside you on a towel or newspaper. And always make sure you have a large pot of fresh water handy for cleaning your brushes and sponges. Now you are ready to begin face painting.

HOW TO PAINT

1. First, apply the base paint. Cover the face with colour using a slightly damp sponge. Your sponge is just damp enough if no water comes out when you squeeze it. If the sponge is too wet the paint will go streaky.

2. Paint on the details with your make-up brushes. Put lighter colours on first.

3. Use a fine (thin) brush for fine lines. Try to keep lines continuous rather than broken and sketchy.

4. Paint carefully round eyes and never get too close with your brush.

5. Ask your model to look up while you paint below the eyes. Your model's eyes should be kept closed while you paint above them.

6. If you don't have the colour you want, mix the paints together to make a new colour. Do this on the back of your hand or in a saucer.

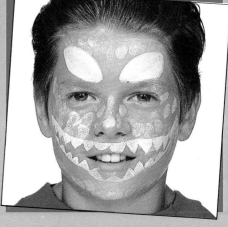

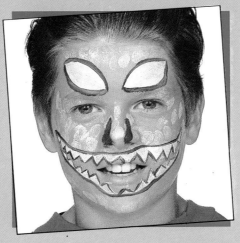

▲ *First, wet your sponge and squeeze out all the water. Dip the sponge into the paint and dab it over the face.*

▲ *Paint on details by drawing the shape you want with a brush then filling it in with the same colour. You can also dab on paint with your fingers.*

◄ *You can make shapes look bolder by outlining – adding a black border around the edge.*

▼ *Use this colour chart to help you mix the colours you need.*

MIX AND MATCH COLOUR CHART

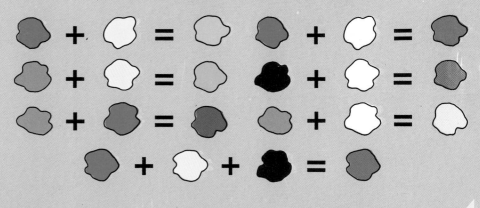

CRAZY CLOWNS

Clowns are always great fun and they're easy to paint. Follow steps 1 to 4 to make a happy clown, or copy the picture on the right to make your clowns look sad. These are the colours you will need for the happy clown:

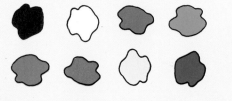

1 First, paint a white base colour over the whole face using a damp sponge.

2 Next, paint large green eyebrows above the eyes using a thick brush.

3 Put a red circle on the end of the nose then paint a smiling, bright red mouth.

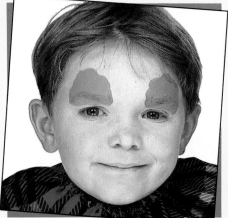

▶ Why not turn your whole hand into a clown? Paint the blue body first, then the white ruffles, head, hands and feet. Add the other details and finish off with the black outline.

▲ Try experimenting with different shapes and colours. Keep your shapes bold and simple and the colours as bright as possible.

4 Using a fine brush, outline the eyebrows in black. Paint white markings on the nose and mouth. Finally, add lots of dots, squiggles and crosses in bright colours (see main picture).

ANIMAL MAGIC

Transform your friends into fun furry animals, such as a teddy bear, rabbit or spotty dog, with one of these designs. Follow steps 1 to 3 to make the cuddly bear face. You will only need three colours:

1 First, paint a light brown base colour over the whole face using a damp sponge.

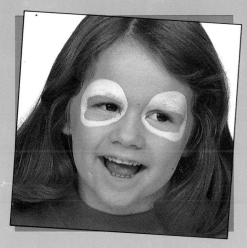

2 Then paint large white circles around the eyes with a brush. Make the circles thicker at the top than at the bottom.

▲ *Here are two more animal faces for you to copy. You'll need to start with a pink base for the rabbit and a white base for the spotty dog. Why not see if you can make up some animal faces of your own!*

3 Using a brush and black paint, add the eyebrows, mouth, nose, and dots for the whiskers.

► *Give yourself a fun tattoo by painting a small animal motif on your arm or leg. Paint the bodies first, then add the black outlines and the details. You'll find lots more crazy creatures on page 30.*

MIGHTY MONSTERS

Terrify your family and friends this Hallowe'en with a fearsome green monster face. It's quick and easy to do — just follow steps 1 to 4.
Here are the colours you will need:

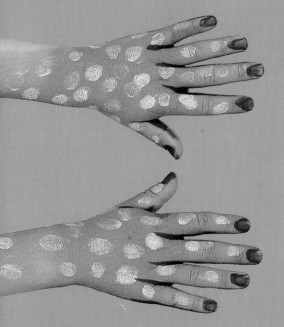

▲ *Do these scary hands to match your monster face. Paint the spots with your fingertips.*

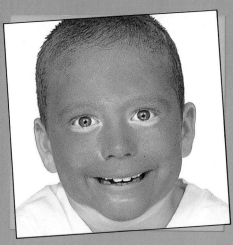

1 Begin by covering the whole face with green paint using a damp sponge. You can colour the hair, too.

2 Add large red eyebrows with a brush. Then paint red markings on the cheeks and beside the eyes.

3 Paint two sharp white fangs at the sides of the mouth and add a flash of white to the eyebrows.

4 Outline the nostrils, lips and fangs in black. Add spiky black brows and finish off with black spots all over.

◄ Just for fun, paint a gruesome ghost or a creepy black vampire bat on your body.

▲ To paint this wicked devil, start with a bright orange base. Then add some fiery yellow eyebrows and red cheeks. Finally, outline the brows, nose and mouth in black.

SNOW QUEEN

Turn your friend into a beautiful snow queen using ice blue paint and a touch of glitter. You can even make a simple crown out of tinsel. Just follow steps 1 to 3 to paint the face. As well as the silver glitter, you only need two other colours:

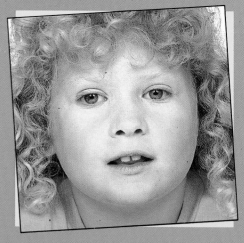

◀ *Paint this fiery gypsy princess using red, yellow, blue and black paints and a little gold glitter. You don't need a base colour for this design. For the final touch, make a gypsy headscarf out of a length of coloured fabric.*

1 Using a damp sponge, cover the whole face in white paint. Now lightly sponge blue paint all round the outside to give a soft blue shadow.

2 Paint broad, spiky eyebrows above the eyes using blue paint and a thick brush.

► *For a finishing touch, give your snow queen a teardrop bracelet and a beautiful diamond ring. A little glitter adds extra sparkle.*

3 Paint the lips blue. Then go over the centre of the lips with white paint, leaving a blue border all round. Carefully paint snow-flake designs on the cheeks with a fine brush. Finish off with silver glitter on the cheeks and brows (see main picture).

IN THE GARDEN

Capture the beauty of a summer garden with these colourful designs. To create a fluttering butterfly, just follow steps 1 to 3.

Here are the colours you will need:

1 Using a damp sponge, paint the top half of the face pink then paint the bottom half yellow. Blend the two colours together where they join.

2 Carefully paint the outline of your butterfly over the eyes, nose and cheeks in blue.

◄ *Decorate your friend's face with flowers and a butterfly to create this pretty garden effect.*

▼ *Turn your friend into a cheeky garden gnome. Paint the red nose and cheeks first using a sponge. Do the white beard and eyebrows with a brush, then add the black details.*

3 Fill in the body and lower wings with white paint. Then add orange tips to the wings. Paint black marks on the lower wings and body, and finish off with two curling antennae (see main picture).

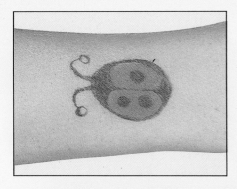

▲ *To paint this lucky ladybird, draw the black outline, fill it in with red, then add black dots.*

DANGEROUS DINOS

Dinosaurs lived over 65 million years ago but you can bring them back to life with this frightening dino face. Just follow steps 1 to 4.

Here are the colours you will need:

1 Using a damp sponge, begin by covering the whole of your model's face with green paint.

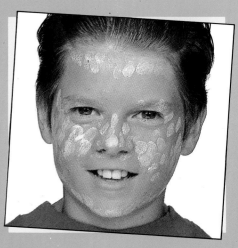

2 Dab splodges of yellow paint over the forehead, nose, cheeks and chin with your fingertips.

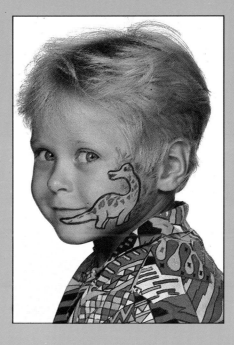

◀ *Instead of painting a dinosaur's face, try painting the whole creature on your model's cheek. Turn to page 30 for another dino idea.*

▼ *Did you know that dinosaur means 'terrible lizard'? Here's one you wouldn't want to meet for real. Sponge the green patches onto a yellow base, then add the details with a brush.*

3 Paint a pair of white eyes on the forehead with a brush. Then paint a wide toothy mouth from ear to ear.

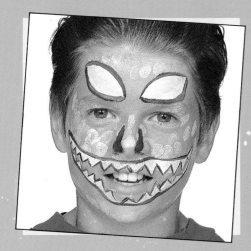

4 Outline the eyes and mouth in black and add large black nostrils. Finish off with red on the eyes and mouth.

19

SAVE THE WORLD

Some of the world's most beautiful animals are in danger of dying out completely. Show your support for endangered animals by painting one of these colourful designs. To paint the tiger, simply follow steps 1 to 3. Here are the colours you will need:

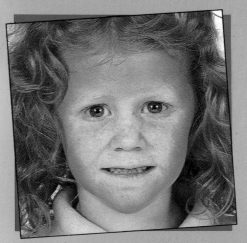

1 Using a damp sponge, cover the whole face with a yellow base. Then sponge orange paint on top of the yellow to make a wide border all round the face.

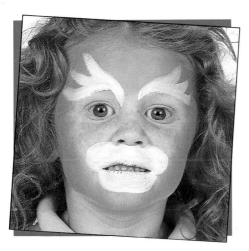

2 Paint a large white muzzle around the mouth and add spiky white eyebrows.

3 Colour in a black nose and mouth. Then outline the eyebrows in black. Finish off with whiskers and lots of tiger stripes.

▲ *Turn your friend into a colourful parrot with this bold design. Try to create a feathered effect with your brush.*

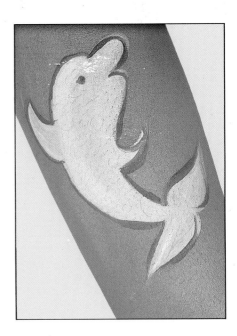

▶ *Paint a fun-loving dolphin on your arm or leg. Can you think of any other endangered animals to paint? See page 30 for more ideas.*

SIMPLY SCENES

Turn your friend's face into a fun picture by creating one of these colourful scenes. Or try making up your own designs instead. How about a jungle scene, a tropical beach or even your own home?

▶ You don't have to paint your scene on someone's face. You can do scenes on hands as well, or even over the whole body.

◀ Paint a chilly Antarctic scene, complete with penguins and icebergs. Sponge on the two base colours first. Then use a brush to paint the jagged white icebergs. Outline the icebergs in black and add a penguin.

► Can you guess which country this is? See if you can make up simple designs for your own or for another country. (This is Holland, in case you didn't know!)

▼ Here's an idea for a pretty country meadow, with bleating lambs, soaring birds and fluffy clouds. Paint the fence at the point where the two base colours meet.

◄ From the icy Antarctic to the scorching hot desert! Sponge bold stripes across the face to look like sand and sky. Then paint a glowing sun and a spiky cactus.

HANDS UP!

The joy of hand painting is that you can do it to yourself — on one hand at least! Here are lots of different designs for you to try. Some of them go with faces in this book. Others are just fun to do on their own.

◄ Once you've painted a face, paint the hands to match. This pretty daisy-chain bracelet goes perfectly with the country meadow design.

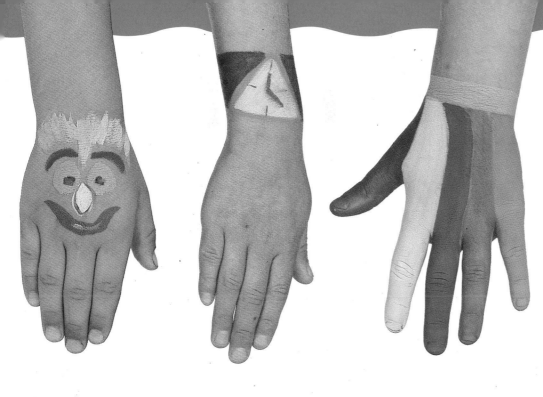

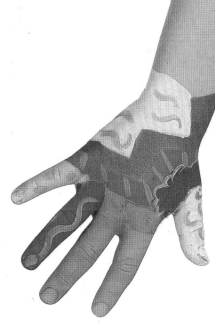

▲ *Practise different designs on your own hand and wrist using lots of bright colours. You can try painting scenes, faces and single motifs, or simply experiment with stripes, spots and zig-zags.*

▼ *These designs go with the faces in the book. The pink glove goes with the snow queen on page 14, the stripy hand matches the tiger on page 20, and the big pink spots are perfect for the clowns on page 8.*

LEGGING IT!

If you don't have the shoes to go with a fancy-dress costume, don't worry. Now you can paint them on instead. Other fun things to paint on legs and feet are animal patterns, socks and scenes.

◀ Fool your friends into thinking you've hurt yourself with these colourful cuts and bruises. They are easy to do with a little red and black paint.

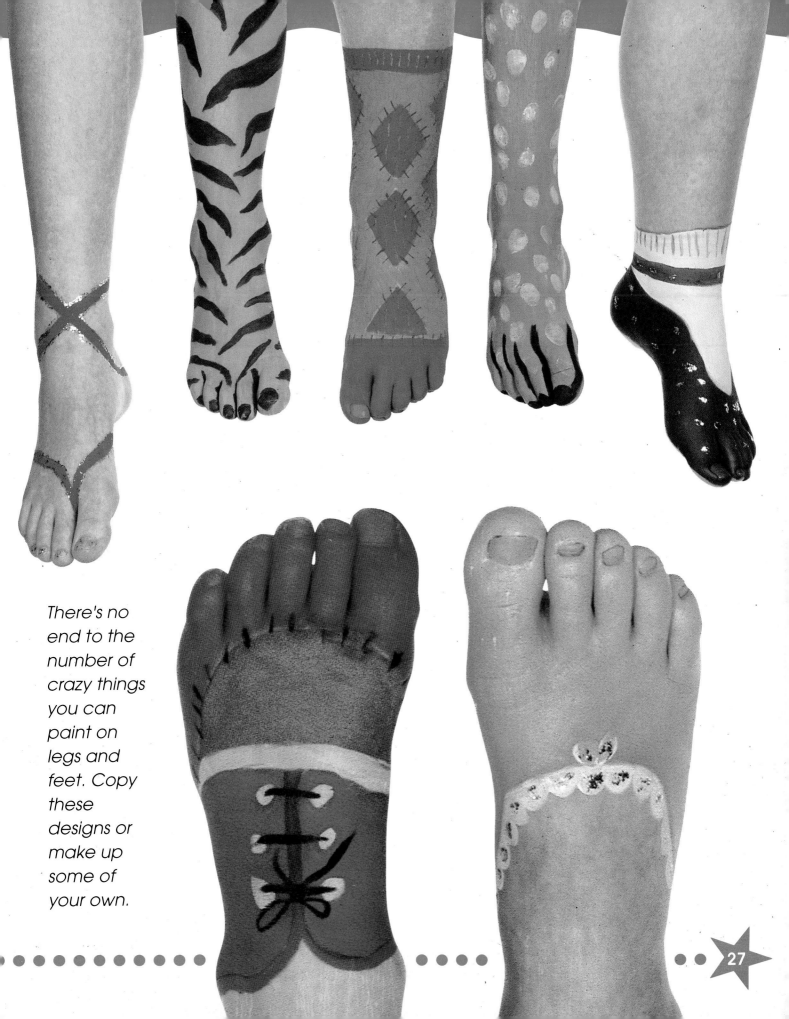

There's no end to the number of crazy things you can paint on legs and feet. Copy these designs or make up some of your own.

OODLES OF DOODLES

▼ A little sun and rain brings out a beautiful rainbow. Add some silver glitter to make the raindrops sparkle.

Here's a host of fun motifs to paint on faces, arms, hands, legs and feet. And don't forget, you can paint the rest of the body, too!

◄ Will our brave warrior free himself from this deadly snake? Paint the yellow base first using a damp sponge. Then sponge a little green on top. Give the snake a black outline, scales and face. Finish off with the red tongue.

◀ It's fun to think up designs for special occasions, such as a firework display, Christmas, a birthday party or Hallowe'en. Turn over the page for more ideas.

▲ Paint this ugly ogre on your hand to scare all your friends.

◀ Garlands of summer flowers make a pretty design for any part of the body. You'll need to use a fine brush and plenty of bright colours. Finish off with a busy bee on the nose.

DOODLES GALORE

Here are lots more fun doodles for you to paint on any part of the body. Some of them go with the face-painting designs in this book. Others are fun to do just on their own. Either paint on the colours then add a fine black outline, or start with the outline and fill in the colours.

▲ Add some **Animal Magic** with these crazy creatures

▲ Have you ever found any of these plants or animals **In the Garden?**

30

▲ Here's another **Dangerous Dino** to add to your collection

▼ Paint these jolly motifs and help **Save the World**

▼ ► Let these magical symbols bring you good luck

Here are more bright ideas for festivals and special occasions

FINISHING TOUCHES

If you are going to a fancy-dress party or acting in a play, you'll need the right costume to go with your face-painting design. And even if you're not, it's still fun to dress up!

Why not start collecting you own dressing-up box? You can ask your friends and family for interesting old clothes, or you can buy them from charity shops and jumble sales. Look out for old hats, scarves, silky and shiny fabrics, sequins, feathers and lace.

Fancy-dress shops and magic shops sell all kinds of false ears and noses, fake moustaches, hats, wigs, masks and glasses. Party hats, too, are worth collecting. Or, why not try making your own hats and masks.

▼ *Keep a box full of old clothes and hats for dressing up.*